Newhaven

in old picture postcards volume 2

by
Peter S. Bailey

European Library - Zaltbommel/Netherlands MCMLXXXIV

About the author:
Peter Bailey came to Newhaven when he was eight years old in 1924 and will forever thank the harbour town for a happy period of growing up until he left in 1937 to join the Surrey Police. On his retirement he moved back to Newhaven in 1963. In 1969 he was a co-founder of the 'Newhaven Historical Society' and since it was opened in 1974, he has been Honorary Curator of the West Foreshore 'Local and Maritime' Museum, owned and operated by this society.

GB   ISBN 90 288 2947 4 / CIP

European Library in Zaltbommel/Netherlands publishes among other things the following series:

IN OLD PICTURE POSTCARDS *is a series of books which sets out to show what a particular place looked like and what life was like in Victorian and Edwardian times. A book about virtually every town in the United Kingdom is to be published in this series. By the end of this year about 175 different volumes will have appeared. 1,250 books have already been published devoted to the Netherlands with the title* **In oude ansichten.** *In Germany, Austria and Switzerland 500, 60 and 15 books have been published as* **In alten Ansichten;** *in France by the name* **En cartes postales anciennes** *and in Belgium as* **En cartes postales anciennes** *and/or* **In oude prentkaarten** *150 respectively 400 volumes have been published.*

For further particulars about published or forthcoming books, apply to your bookseller or direct to the publisher.

This edition has been printed and bound by Grafisch Bedrijf De Steigerpoort in Zaltbommel/Netherlands.

INTRODUCTION

Rather than give a lenghty account of the History of Newhaven, I have attempted to incorporate much of it in the explanatory captions to the photographs, whereby certain facts and incidents can be readily associated to the present day scene.

Newhaven, like so many other coastal towns, had its defences on high ground from ancient times, with emphasis on the protection of the bay and the river estuary. At some time the river moved to Seaford and made an exit at the eastern end of the coastline. During the reign of Queen Elizabeth I this limb of the Cinque Port of Hastings, became choked and finally broke out in an area west of the 'Buckle', this was named the New Haven. The whole district was very marshy and many channels were formed and deserted, one of these later becoming the creek to Tidemills. This sluggish situation led to much flooding in the Ouse valley up to Lewes, the low land at times being unusable for grazing, even in the summer. This situation became so serious that the length south from the present swing bridge was straightened and cut to the sea, emerging under Castle Hill. This is believed to be the course of the Ouse in Roman times. The canal work eased the flooding upstream and a fixed harbour entrance was eventually established. The old Saxon name of 'Meeching' was dropped and the fishing village by the river bank became Newhaven.

The coming of the railway in 1847 was directly connected with the introduction of a steam packet service to Dieppe. The routes were extended over the years to include St. Malo, Honfleur and Caen. Also, there were regular cargo-passenger services to this harbour by steamers from St. Nazaire and the Clyde. The freights handled by all these vessels, added to the regular passenger and cargo sailings to and from Dieppe resulted in the 1880's with Newhaven becoming the sixth most important port in the United Kingdom in terms of revenue earned.

Three other milestones were to follow, the first was the New Cut made in 1863, when yet another canal was made, this time north from the area of the first swing bridge (yet to be built) later to become North Quay. As a result of this work Denton Island was formed. With the spoil from the New Cut, Pennants Eye, a backwater reaching almost to the town railway station, was filled in. These extensive alterations created an increased flushing effect by the faster moving water. The next major happening was in 1879 when the creek to Tidemills was closed allowing the building of East Quay and in this year began the dramatic Harbour Works which included the widening of the harbour mouth, the building of new east and west piers and the reclaiming of the area under the Fort Cliffs to create the promenade, this whole massive enterprise culminating in the construction of the remarkable breakwater and the establishing of a cross channel service free of tidal restrictions.

With the diverting of the railway track supplying the breakwater, to a new course around Sleepers Hole at the turn of the century, the causeway running from the lifeboat station to the Green Light was removed for a considerable length and with much dredging an area of this slob land was deepened to allow for a lay-by berth to accommodate two cross channel steamers abreast and moorings for two dredgers plus any yachts which could squeeze in. Destroyers were moored here during the First World War and a loading area for tank landing craft in the Second World War.

The deep mud to the south and north was not removed until the yacht marina development of the 1960's. Apart from the renewal of quays and piers (and a new swing bridge in the 1970's) there were few other changes in the port scene in the period covered by this book.

The growth of the town went hand in hand with the progress of the port. Industry was not encouraged, there were small concerns like the chalk quarry and the even smaller 'blue boulder' trade, when hand picked beach flints were collected and sent to Runcorn for use in glass and pottery glazing processes. The building of sailing ships of several hundred tons had taken place in the shipyards between the 'old river' and now Robinson Road, but after the heyday of John Gray the quest for steam driven iron craft, put the trade into decline by the mid-1800's. A small fishing industry has fortunately survived.

Newhaven town has been stripped of all its old properties and its few impressive houses have been demolished, leaving but the record of the one time existance of a Roman villa in the area of the present police station, and apart from the possible inclusion of the 'Bridge Inn' of 1623 there remains only the delightful old Parish Church of St. Michael as the sole reminder that once a place called 'Meeching' was hereabouts. The greatest 'incident' of the last war occurred at 5 a.m. on 22nd November 1944, when a barge carrying 180 tons of a very high explosive broke from its tow and came ashore on the west stone beach, here it hit a mine and blew itself up and but for the cliffs, much of Newhaven would have followed it. Windows were broken in Lewes 7 miles away... The mess in Newhaven can be imagined, an additional problem was the loss of so much rationed food through the contamination by splintered glass both in the homes and the shops. Emergency feeding had to be introduced. Injuries were numerous with many of the population being awakened by their ceilings joining them in bed, yet only one person was killed, a wall fell on an unfortunate naval rating.

Compiling this, the second book of 'Newhaven in old picture postcards' has been a most pleasing task, tinged with the sadness at having to reject so many other lovely or constructive pictures. I have attempted to concentrate on scenes of places which have gone or been greatly altered, this will explain the omission of our parish church and the restored Fort Newhaven. Reference is sometimes made to volume 1 and a picture number, this is to help readers who have the first book to link up the cross references. In no way is this intended as a sales promotion as there is no certainty for how long volume 1 will be available.

Since the formation of the Newhaven Historical Society in 1969 thousands of photographs have been given or loaned for copying. This unique collection is housed in the Society's Museum at the West Foreshore and from these archives I have made the selection of pictures featured in this book.

May I take this opportunity to thank all of those who have so kindly contributed towards this store of local history. Several of the photos will have passed through many hands, so that it would be impossible to be sure to whom to give acknowledgement and likewise there is always the fear of accidently infringing on some reproduction rights. I hope sincerely that this has been avoided.

Lastly may I thank all of the members of this Society for their support which has ensured our survival after many years and my sincere appreciation to the officers, past and present for their work and generous sacrifice of their free time. I think it can be justly said: 'We have done Newhaven proud!'

Peter S. Bailey

1. The Shepherds Cottage, Church Hill, just below the junction with now Newfield Road. It is said that the roof 'departed' in the same storm in December 1867 which wrecked the Chain Pier at Brighton. The last private owner, Miss Caroline Catt, died on 14th November 1895. She had bought 'Meeching Place' from William Elphick on 29th September 1865. Transference to the Convent Order was on 14th July 1896. Caroline Catt was a daughter of the famous miller at Tidemills, William Catt, who had in his time been an adviser to King Louis Philippe on milling matters so it is no surprise to learn that Caroline attended upon the fugitive French Monarch and his Queen, during their one night stay at the 'Bridge' Hotel.

French Convent. Newhaven.
Badminton Court.

2. In 1912 one of the young lady boarders at the Convent sent this card to her parents in France. By courtesy of the recent craze for postcard collecting it has found its way back to this country. It would seem that the badminton court was also the croquet lawn! The Convent was built on the site of the 1591 'Meeching Place', the last resident was Miss Caroline Catt. On each first of May, the town's children would assemble in the grounds each carrying a garland of flowers, the footmen and gardeners would position the youngsters and then Miss Catt would emerge and give each an orange, a bun and one penny.

3. Annual Corpus Christi procession from the Convent in Church Hill, to the Catholic Church in Fort Road, 1930's.

4. Looking down Church Hill in about 1919. The Baptist Chapel is on the left. The gates, right, are at the entrance to the Convent of the Sacred Heart. This day and boarding school was built on the site of the 1591 'Meeching Place'. The front face of the old house can be seen in volume 1 picture 19. It was pulled down and a second school block erected on the plot. The arrangement is little changed today apart from the mode of occupation.

5. Upper High Street in 1891. The Webbers Farm Gate on the left is in the area of the present day post office. Wellcourt Farm is on the right. (vol. 1, pic 15.)

6. An early view outside Wellcourt Farm, upper High Street, south side. The postman, near the gas lamp, probably knew the names of the entire population at that time.

22 NEWHAVEN. — High Street from the Top. — 22

7. Upper High Street in about 1910. An open tiered bus trundles down the main road. The floor of the vehicle was on an upward slope towards the rear, the passengers all having a good forward view in consequence. The bus is abreast of todays Lloyds Bank.

8. At the junction of High Street with Meeching Road was S. Thompson the grocer, baker and ironmonger. Just around the corner, in Marshall Lane, his brother baked the bread. The accommodation above the shop has served as the local headquarters of the Liberal and Labour parties. Now of course, the venue of a well known school of dancing.

9. In the Marshall Lane Bakery, Ben Thompson poses beside the balance scales. A lovely example of 'how things were'.

10. 'Sussex Lodge', High Street, facing into Meeching Road, a parade of shops is now on this site. In 1871 this was Albert School, a grammar school for boys, day and boarding. The name can be seen above 'Sussex Lodge' over the entrance. In this year William Castle Leaver was proprietor and headmaster. There were three teaching staff, one governess, 25 pupils, 7 domestic staff. By 1881 the school was at 34 Meeching Road, down to 8 pupils, 2 teachers and 2 domestics. By this time Dr. Thomas Martyn Cann had taken over 'Sussex Lodge', which was demolished in 1961 having housed other doctors and a cinema proprietor during the interim period.

11. Looking down the High Street from the junction with Meeching Road, in the early 1920's. The old silent cinema is showing 'The Kid' featuring Charlie Chaplin and Jackie Coogan. This cinema was superseded by the 'Kinema' also silent, which was between Marshall Lane and 'Saxonholme' (later to be the town's fire station). With the coming of the talkies, the 'Cinema de Luxe' as shown here was enlarged and refurbished. Note the boy outside with his metal hoop.

12. Corbetts Shop, right, offers apart from Sunlight Soap, 'Lloyds News' a bird cage and 'Tit Bits' (recently defunct) offering 'Confessions of a Beer House Keeper'! A poster near the lady at the left, betrays the date of 1891. Next shop is Noakes the grocer later to be the first International Stores and today, Boots the Chemist. Next door is Reeves the stationers and post office, now the Midland Bank. Beyond is the house 'Homestreu' with finally the Whitehart Hotel as positioned before the 1925 cut back.

13. The High Street looking east in about the 1870's/80's. The pram near left is at the entrance to Albion Place, a passage running up the side of the 'Blue Anchor' Public House. A lot of this area was cleared with the rebuilding of the cinema, but at one time a Mr. Wood ran a school at the top of the passageway. That a person living in the street is ill, is indicated by the straw spread over the road to muffle the sounds of horses hooves and wheels. The 'victim' lived to the right, just out of the picture, but it is said that in this particular instance, he was in debt, so he pulled down his bedroom blinds, set the story going and 'did a bunk'.

14. Bannisters had shops on both sides of the High Street, hence the likening of the street to a stairway. The branch here commemorating a Queen Victoria jubilee, is the site of todays Woolworths store.

15. Looking down the High Street probably in the 1870's. The barn like building near right has yet to make way for the first Barclays Bank. The boxes on the footpath would be at the junction with South Lane, this was a collecting point for the two (horse and waggon) carriers operating to Brighton, J. Sheppard and S. Noakes, on Tuesdays and Fridays. On Wednesdays and Saturdays R. Reynolds would collect at the same point for goods going to Lewes. To the left of the 'Bridge' Hotel can be seen the shore end of the old draw bridge with the toll house beside it. The fee for humans to cross was one half penny, the same as for an Ass! Denton residents were exempted of charge in consideration of their maintaining the Long Drove. Captain Tothill's house can be seen on the left.

16. From 'Oxleys Corner'. On the left The London and County Bank, now 'Natwest'. The small shop on the right is a bakers, but in the centre Mr. J. Webber is proud to announce that the 'Ship' Hotel not only sells Tamplins Brews, but that choice wines, spirits and cigars may be obtained. Billiards it seems can also be played. To the right of the name Webber, the wording appears to say 'Carriages and Horses on site'.

17. Looking up the High Street from the 'Bridge' Hotel in about 1890 with the 'Ship' Hotel extreme right. Some of the houses have yet to become shops or offices. Beyond the hand cart a small derelict building has yet to make way for the first Barclays Bank.

18. Looking up the High Street in 1880. On the facing wall of the building leading into St. Lukes Lane we read that the shop below is a fruiterers and green grocers run by J.W. Lower. The nearest shop, right, is a butchers.

19. St. Lukes Lane, northern end. In this picture, St. Lukes Cottages and Florence Place are behind the camera on the left side. In front, on the left, are 'Cairo Cottages' and 'Inkerman Cottages'. The lane commenced beside now Woolworths and ended at the junction with Essex Place. Straight ahead can be seen Robinson Road. Essex Place disappeared with the Northway construction. The 'Blacksmiths Arms' Public House was behind and below the cottages right.

20. The 'Blacksmiths Arms' riverside, about 1912. Cars turning off Northway into the car park, must cross over the site of this public house. There was a blacksmiths forge next door cornering with St. Lukes Lane. The strange structure left is the upturned bow half of a boat which was adapted into a gents toilet, conveniently sited on the river bank. The landlady Mrs. Judith Coleman is the figure to the right.

21. Essex Place, alias 'The swine pit' or later 'Cocksparrow'. This ran from the bottom of Folly Hill, Lewes Road, around approximately the route of Northway, finishing at the 'Blacksmiths Arms'. The roofs of the houses in Lower Place can be seen above the near houses and there is a glimpse of St. Lukes Lane in the left distance. The picture was taken from the southern end of Elphick Road, itself since shortened.

22. A military funeral cortege makes its way along South Road to the cemetery. There are records of several smallpox and even flu epidemics and it is probable that a soldier from the Fort has succombed to one of these. The Primitive Methodist Chapel, left, later became the 'Shakespeare Hall', then a boys club and is presently a business premises.

23. Drain laying, South Road. An observation of workers and onlookers in the early 1920's. A fraction of the 'Volunteer' Inn can be seen at the near right. The picture was taken from an upstairs class room at the girls school.

24. 'Sussex Place', this is now under Southway and the adjoining Health Centre Car Park. One would walk down Church Road, beside Christ Church (police station now on this site) across Chapel Street and into Sussex Place. At the far end, one turned left along the twitten emerging beside the 'Crown' Hotel in Bridge Street (see vol. 1, pic. 34).

25. Chapel Street, believed early 1920's. Left to right, Billy Norman with delivery trap, Harry Dann, family butcher and Fred Nash. The business was established in 1882. These premises are now occupied by Joan Lampon, estate agent.

26. Chapel Street, south from Bridge Street. The old Congregational Chapel, right, had been Amy Bros. garage before they moved to their new premises at the top of the High Street (vol. 1, pic. 16. Correction to make of car in this picture. It was a 'Chenard Walcker'). Previously, the old chapel had housed the 'Electric Theatre' an early silent picture house. Today the aroma of frying fish and chips pervades the air.

27. Rear of the old cobbled cottages in Chapel Street. These were opposite the 'Jolly Sailor' public house (vol. 1, pic. 32). Note the rear of the infants school, far right.

28. Bridge Street, probably soon after the First World War. Hedges the greengrocer is at the left, in the far centre can be seen a fish costermongers barrow. This location was to become the main stop for the Brighton buses until the advent of the ring road. In the background is the tripod crane, 'Sheerlegs', next the 'Crown' Hotel. Nearest right is the 'Cromwell Cyclists Rest', which at one time occupied the site of the present Conservative Club. Beneath the coffee tavern is Woolgars passage, which ended at the 'Jolly Sailor' in Chapel Street.

29. A delightful scene outside Bannisters, Ship Chandlers and Bakers in Bridge Street.

30. Staff outside the 1904 post office in Meeching Road (where is now Dacre Road leading to the car park). Near left is a stand pipe for filling the water cart to sprinkle the roads when dry and dusty. Trees flourish in the gardens of 'Willowhale' left (now a dental surgery) and 'Saxonholme' right. The Congregational Chapel, centre, was built in 1856 with 'sittings for 500' (vol. 1, pic. 34).

31. Although nicknamed 'Piano Street', before all of the houses were built Meeching Road was called 'Prospect Place'. This photo of about 1882 was taken from the southern end and looks over Meeching Court Farm. The area beyond and right was known as 'The Moneyburghs' (and later 'New Jerusalem'). The flat field near the harbour was called 'Huggets Field' and was in fact used by the pupils of the Albert School ('Sussex Lodge') for their sports days, which included swimming races in the river. The continuous causeway south from the lifeboat house, can be seen, also the concrete mixer at East Quay (vol. 1, pic. 41).

32. 'The path divides'- the boy from his dream, to go to sea. His choice in this case would be P & A Campbell's pleasure steamer 'Brighton Queen' 2, or the 'Dieppe Screw', 'Rennes' or her sister 'Bordeaux'. Here photographed in the mid-1930's this path connecting Fort Road with the harbour side was the route taken by the cattle from Meeching Court Farm (now flats) to graze at Tidemills, crossing at low water on a chalk bed laid down between stages 11 and 12. It is difficult to visualise no development on the east side, but it was so before 1847.

33. The old 'Hope' Inn, not a rush for free beer, but a fishing competition weigh-in, 1920's/30's. The solid tyred car is a 'Trojan'. The two cottages, left, were absorbed into the rebuilt 'Hope' of the 1930's.

34. Paradise-Newhaven! Late 1920's. The weekend and holiday beach chalets between the promenade and the cliffs, extending almost to the west pier. With so much else, they disappeared with the last war. Healthy as seaside living may be, a fever with its local 'cure' persisted through the last century, this was 'The Ague'. Onto a piece of paper to be hung around the neck was written: 'Ague, ague, I thee defy, three days shiver, three days shake, make us well for Jesus sake.' The paper had to be left until it fell off, by which time the patient was deemed cured!

35. Kingpin of survival for Port Newhaven, the wonderful and very necessary 'Breakwater'. Building commenced in 1879 and was completed by 1893. The length is 2,700 feet. In this picture the structure is still very new and the 'Fricker' rocks, right, have not yet been covered by shingle (vol. 1, pics. 39 to 46).

36. Sleepers Hole in about 1880. Left is the Fort Gunners house, demolished in the 1970's. At centre is the 'Ark' house (vol. 1, pic. 3) showing bedroom windows in the hull. This semi-detached wooden building with slate roof was constructed on a 16 ton barge built at Rye in 1813 and later brought here by J.H. Bull. Left on a spring tide, it was surrounded by infill when the railway line was brought around the 'Hole' to the breakwater. Beyond the 'Ark' are three of the 'Shants' (Shanties) used by the navvies engaged in the 1879 harbour works, above these, the coastguard houses. Near right, pickled sleepers are taken away by limber. Pier and quayside piles were known as 'sleepers' the word later being adopted for the shorter ones used on the railways.

37. The old Customs boatmans watch house, left, was just north of the lifeboat house, this area was known as 'Blackmans Head'. The tall flag pole passes through 'Lorraine' in Fort Road, one of Newhaven's few attractive houses, which was demolished and the present fire station built on the site. Three trucks from the chalk quarry can also be seen. Visible are the old cottages at the bottom of Hillside and the semi detached houses 'Seaview' at the entrance to Chapel Street, demolished after bomb damage in the Second World War. Pile drivers in the 'New Cut', suggest work has started on the North Quay.

38. Topsail schooner 'Flying Foam' abreast of the harbour watch house 1920's/30's. She is on her way to Every's wharf at Piddinghoe with a cargo of pig iron for the Lewes foundry. The dredger, left, is the 'Newey' ex 'Cambois'. The channel steamer is the 'Dieppe' (1905-1933) which was to become a replacement yacht for Lord Moyne after his loss of 'Brighton IV'. As M.Y. 'Rosaura' the old 'Dieppe' cruised in the Mediterranean hosting the Prince of Wales and Mrs. Simpson. She was lost on war service and the 'Flying Foam' perished in a storm.

39. A delightful harbour scene in about 1885. The inner of the two far sailing vessels is the Newhaven built and registered 'Sussex Maid'. The near cargo steamer at Railway Quay is the 'screw' 'Newhaven 2', (1875-1899) and beyond, the funnel of 'Lyon' or sister 'Italie'.

40. West Bank about 1888. Bow of the 'Sussex Maid' left. The boat with two men is 'Albertine 1' an ex-Hastings beach pleasure craft (a second was to follow) owned by R.R. Collard. She would be sailed round to Old Nore area, grounded and when tide had receded the crew would load her with 'blue boulders', these would be dumped on harbour side, as in photo, until enough for a cargo when they would be transhipped on such as the 'Aldersons' of Sunderland (behind) to Runcorn, where in small boats the flints were sent to various potteries where they were burnt in kilns and then crushed. This powder, mixed with clay, was said to improve the whiteness of the earthenware.

41. Blue boulder pickers on the west beach about 1927. Tom Winder and his sister Elizabeth (later Harvey) pose with their carrying baskets. The flints in this case were loaded into railway trucks, for the potteries, the pickers receiving four shillings and sixpence per ton! Tom did the lifting for his sister. In the summertime he might have been operating a rowing ferry between the green lights, he might be accompanying, with his accordion, Gracie Fields with a sing-song at the Hotel Peacehaven or just providing the music for one of his brothers with a dancing doll, in one of the local pubs. Elizabeth made a good contribution too, he still serves on the ferry 'Senlac'!

42. From the Bonded Warehouse looking across West Quay to Railway Quay early this century. The near tug is the 'Belle of the Usk'. Two 'Dieppe screws' are unloading abreast of the 'London and Paris' Hotel. The water tower for the East Quay hydraulic cranes can be seen above the cargo boat, left.

43. South from the old swing bridge about 1910. The steamers left to right, the sleek 'Sussex', built in 1896 to replace the illfated 'Seaford' (vol. 1, pic. 68) which was sunk in 1895 within a year of construction through a collission in fog with the Joint Services' own cargo steamer 'Lyon' (no loss of life). 'Sussex' was torpedoed in the First World War, with many casualties, but was later salved. Next is the pleasure steamer 'Sussex Belle' and nearest right the beautiful and last paddler, 'Paris III'.

44. Newhaven's first motor fire engine, a solid tyred 'Fiat', an ex-Brighton machine. Here 1920's/30's outside the Council Offices in Fort Road, where the engine was kept in what is now the Council Chamber. Quite an amount of protection could be anticipated close to the harbour, by virtue of the powerful firefighting equipment fitted to the two tugs. In fact the 'Hauler' went all of the way to Lewes town bridge to assist at the fire at the 'Beare' Hotel.

45. The girls school in the old Dacre Road at the junction with South Lane in about 1912. To the left is the old Police station and previously to this the law was upheld from a house in South Road. The multi-story car park occupies the site of the school today, but before this grand building for the girls was constructed there had been an infants school here and a mixed school (where the girls sat in front and the boys behind) to the right, this was to be replaced by an infants school, itself a victim of 'Southway'. This reshuffle came about with the building of the boys school. There was also an infants school in Railway Road.

46. Teachers at Meeching Boys School in about 1927. Rear, left to right: Messrs Ray, Rogers, Larwill, Burt, Pratt, Akehurst and Cox. Front, left to right: Miss Curry, Messrs. Hodges, Bullbeck, E.J. Coker (headmaster) Maguire and Marson and Miss Marks. Some of these fine people are happily still with us in 1984.

A. Saunders   D. Scrase   J. Brown   H. Adams   F. Richardson   F. Holman
Mr Lapierre   H. Kennedy   P. Saunders   W. Feist   Mr E J Coker
R. Howard   H. Cornford   A. Aitken

47. Newhaven Boys School, Champions, East Sussex Football League 1930-31 season. Matches played 11, won 11, goals for 109, against 2! Team captain Percy Saunders was later to be signed on by Sunderland FC. but the last war deprived this young hopeful of a chance to fame. His was the supreme sacrifice. Mr. Lapierre, left, teacher, coach and later a Councillor, well deserves the street named after him. At right is Mr. E.J. Coker, headmaster and great supporter of his young wizards; he was a strict but fair and very respected man. He tamed the naughtiest into admiring him.

48. Henry Arhtur Towner (Towner Bros.- Stone & Towner, etc., successors to the Tipper Brewery) is said to have owned the first motor car in Newhaven, a Mercedes Benz. Here his wife to be, 16½ year old Winifred Stone poses at the controls whilst Henry takes the picture in the Brighton Road in 1900.

CORONATION AT NEWHAVEN

49. Fortunately, many photos were taken of the procession through the town to commemorate the coronation of King George V. In this picture taken from an upstairs window on the 'Bridge' Hotel, can be seen, left, the corner of The London and County Bank. The nearest lady, right, is Mrs. Winifred Towner (nee Stone) with her first child Mary. Mrs. Towner as a teenager is featured in the picture of the first car in Newhaven.

50. Britannia takes a ride on Newhaven's no. 1 vehicle of the day, a horse drawn manual fire engine. This with a ladder escape on wheels was housed in what is now the Council Chamber. The picture was taken from the recreation ground with the fence of Sleepers Hole behind. The occasion being celebrated is the coronation of King George V.

H.M.H.S. 'BRIGHTON'

51. S.S. 'Brighton' (4) here as a hospital carrier in the First World War. Built in 1903 she was the first turbine steamer on this route. An 'eventful' vessel she was in collision (5/6th November 1912) with the worlds largest full rigged sailing ship, the German 'Preussen', the latter becoming a total loss after running ashore near Dover. 'Brighton' was held responsible, the Captain lost his 'ticket' and later shot himself. King George V and U.S. President Wilson, both travelled the channel on this ferry. In 1929 on a winter night crossing she arrived at Dieppe with her bridge damaged by heavy seas and her upper-works and even rigging, festooned in icicles. The mail had to get through! She was sold in 1930 and converted into the luxury yacht 'Rousalka' for Lord Moyne of the Guiness family. Remarkably, she cruised as far as the west coast of Canada, but sadly was later wrecked on the coast of Ireland.

52. The First World War, troops on parade in the recreation ground. Newhaven was a sealed military town, the adult residents being issued with a registration certificate and photograph, without which, re-entry couldn't be made. Soldiers were billeted about the town as well as at the Fort and at the camp which can just be discerned in the Hillcrest Road area in the picture. Note also a corner of the lake at the right of photo and the few houses in Gibbon Road.

53. An air picture from the First World War, looking across Sleepers Hole. Note Destroyers, the old Watch House, Transports at the East and Railway Quays, the 'London' and 'Paris' Hotel and the numerous allotments at East Side (Turkey Town). Newhaven was one of the main supply ports for the western front. At times Transports were three abreast at East Quay and singly at Railway and North Quays. Small naval craft were mostly at the West Bank stages.

54. The east side of the harbour lined with transports in the First World War. At the West Bank are moored escort trawlers, but outermost is the steam hopper 'Trident'. which was built to lay the foundations of the breakwater in 1879. Near are two coal barges used for bunkering ships, each coalie with his basket of coal walked up one set of steps out of the hold and then up another (which can be seen) into the side doors of the ship, to the bunkers, tipped out his coal and repeated the process, several hours very hard work.

55. First World War, loading supplies for the western front, at East Quay. Female labour was introduced for this work. Extensive feeding arrangements had to be made for the vast influx in numbers. A special train was run daily from Brighton, picking up at Lewes. This was known as 'The Lousy Lou', with no prizes for guessing why! Sent to France were 440 guns, 15,300 vehicles, 2,682,800 tons of ammunition, 921,300 tons of ordnance stores, 2,207,300 tons of supplies, stores returned 743,200 tons. As a sideline: about 10,000 troops. There were 8,330 sailings of transports with eleven ships lost, the memorial to the crews of these remains almost unnoticed at West Quay, south from the swing bridge. All of this tonnage was moved long before the days of fork lift trucks and 'Ro-Ro' ships.

56. No radios to give out the news in those days, but an attentive gathering listens to an announce-ment declaring the end of hostilities in 1918. The address is being made from the 'New Bridge' Inn, which is now a sports shop. Where the timber is stacked, ran the rail line which connected the main line with the end of the breakwater. Behind is the bridge keepers hut and to the right, the Missions to Seamen's Chapel. Behind the chapel can be seen the Royal Engineers Drill Hall, with on the roof an advert for Towner Bros. Bottled Beers (successors to Tipper Ales).

57. The 1918 peace comes to Denton and it would seem that the total population has turned out to follow the Reverend Kimpson in the procession of appreciation through the lovely village.

58. The Royal Naval Volunteer Reserve Drill Hall in Bridge Street with rear access to 'Washers' wharf. This was part of the last war shore base H.M.S. 'Forward'. The majority of this building disappeared with the construction of North Way, leaving but little more than the frontage. Here were created champion gymnasts and whaler rowing crews. As the flags suggest it was also the venue for many happy dancing feet. Three drill halls, with their potential for entertainment, have gone since the Second World War.

59. The suspense is over, the dreaded war is now under way as the poster boards declare outside of Tom White's newsagents in Bridge Street. 1945 was a long way off. The shop has now been incorporated into a social club, but the premises are on the site of Towner Bros. steam flour mill, a tall reminder of which still stands unoccupied next door. In its day, the mill replaced the last Newhaven windmill which stood on Meeching Downs at the top of Church Hill. It was dismantled and re-erected at Chailey where it can still be seen in the grounds of Chailey Heritage.

60. From the 'Hope' Inn, early 1940. Newhaven was the no. 1 ambulance port for the British Expeditionary force, with hospital ships based here which were to bring back thousands of casualties to the U.K. from the channel ports and the beaches of Dunkirk. Our steamer 'Paris' (IV) under captain Ernie Biles with his local crew and nursing staff, crept between a minefield and the beach in such shallow water that her own wash overtook her, yet she got into Calais and was the last hospital carrier to leave. Subsequently she made a run into the harbour at Dunkirk and two later trips to the entrance pier. The 'Paris' brought home 740 patients. On 2nd June 1940 she sailed from Deal Roads, again for the beaches, but at 7.15 p.m. a wave of planes bombed and machine gunned her, her main steam pipe burst and two crew were to die. She was bombed again at 8.00 p.m. and then abandoned. The noble 'Paris' sank. Such exploits deserve recognition.

61. War time fire fighting equipment ready for inspection by Councillors Alan and Bob Bannister with town clerk Mainwood between them and E.J. Coker (hands on hips). At strict attention is the then fire chief, R. Stanley Gray, in normal times the local optician. The parade is taking place beside the boys school and facing Bay Vue. Also included were A.R.P. ambulance crews with some lady drivers.

62. A demonstration of Newhaven's anti-invasion defences, looking south from the swing bridge on 12th January 1942. Oil was poured onto the water between the East and West piers at the 'narrows', this was ignited by flame throwers and would no doubt have discouraged the most ardent supporter of Adolf Hitler to attempt an entry into the harbour. Subsequently oil storage tanks were installed at the eastern end of the dry moat at the Fort and even more elaborate defences of this type were prepared for the protection of the bay and its beach.

63. Landing craft personnel arriving at Newhaven for employment in the tragic one-day-raid on Dieppe to occur in the early morning of 19th August 1942. Many of these boats were hidden under a camouflaged framework across the river south of Piddinghoe between the two ends of a by-passed Ox Bow on the eastern side, thus avoiding the possible interpretation by a reconnaissance pilot that the river abruptly disappeared for a distance. In the centre of the picture can be seen the Fort drill hall with the air sea rescue crews quarters above.

64. From the now Ferry Berth towards the old harbour watch house. A steam gun boat makes its way to sea, above her foredeck can be seen a number of tank landing craft, stern on, in Sleepers Hole. Most of the ramp laid for loading these vessels remains today. Despite being an attractive target to the enemy, Newhaven suffered only 117 high explosive bombs, 4 oil bombs, 290 incendiaries and 2 flying bombs. Fifteen people were killed and 47 injured. Maybe the decoy of the harbour lights, set up in the sea end of the Cuckmere valley, did provide a diversion!

65. A deadly 'fish' is loaded onto motor torpedoe boat no. 250 of the 14th M.T.B. Flotilla at the East Quay (H.M.S. 'Agressive') between July 1943 and May 1944. Her Commander, Geoffrey Baker, centre of the figures on the quay, left, was unaware that the picture had been taken until the visit of the yacht 'Medyna' (ex. M.T.B. 253) on Friday 21st August 1981, for the Coastal Forces Veterans Association re-union. M.T.B. 253 was also based here and is the last sea going craft of her type.

66. 'Oxleys (Baldwins) Corner'. 'Wings for Victory' week, Saturday 19th to 26th June 1943. Navy lasses of the W.R.N.S., march smartly from Bridge Street into High Street. Note the anti-splinter tape on the shop windows. There were several such fund raising events for the war effort: 'Spitfire' week, 'Warship' week and so on. The East Quay and the 'London and Paris' Hotel was H.M.S. 'Agressive', the R.N.V.R. Drill Hall, the Guiness Trust Houses, with the hidden underground control centre, was H.M.S. 'Forward'. Fort Road, including the 'Sheffield Arms' Hotel was H.M.S. 'Newt', being mostly concerned with the tank landing craft based in Sleepers Hole.

67. 'Storm harvest' – 13th March 1914. The brigantine 'Catherine', right, was to become just debris on the beach within a few days, she missed the harbour when making a run for safety. On the other hand, the Thames sailing barge 'Jachin', abreast of Bishopstone Tidemills, was to be refloated and refitted. As late as the 1970's she was (and still maybe) around as the barge yacht 'Venta', an indication of her stout construction.

68. The French steamer 'Rouen' leaves about 1928 for Dieppe in an atmosphere of power and potential speed and such would be the case, for she would arrive at her home port 3 hours and ten minutes later. She was built in 1912 and is here coal burning, her funnels have been shortened and bridge work raised if compared with the earlier picture of her sister 'Newhaven' (vol. 1, pic. 75). In the First World War she was torpedoed when serving as a naval scout, she was abandoned, then retrieved and repaired. She and her sister were both converted to oil burning, single funnels and plated in promenade decks in the early 1930's. Worn out by the Germans in the Second World War, they never returned to service and were scrapped.

69. The 8th July 1938 brought excitement to onlookers as they watched the tug 'Foremost 22' try and assist the 'Rouen' back into the entrance channel. This was achieved after ¾ of an hour and one broken tow rope. In strong southwesterlies the surge around the end of the breakwater can spell trouble for vessels entering, particularly at low water. At one time the channel steamers were fitted with a foresail which could be quickly released to compensate this tendancy to turn. 'Paris IV' of 1913 was originally fitted with such a sail, despite her ability to have made the crossing in 2 hours and 36 minutes! But that sort of record speed was achieved in ideal conditions.

70. The third day of July 1911: a day to remember at Heighton. During a circuit of Europe Air Race, in the final leg, Calais-Dover-Shoreham-Hendon, a participant M. Train, brought his flimsy monoplane down to check his location. Unfortunately his machine rolled backwards damaging its tail on a fence and putting him out of the competition.

71. Dual perpetuity in one picture! Who could have ever imagined when this photo was taken in the mid-1930's that the locomotive the 'Fenchurch' would still be running in 1984, albeit on the 'Bluebell' Railway. A short length of track is still beneath the flyover, from where she left the main line to venture as far as the end of the breakwater. Preceeding her with red flag and bell (as required on a roadway) is Mr. Harry Avis, town councillor in his day, little could he have imagined that not only was a road to be named after him, but also a large industrial estate!

Denton Near Newhaven. 2654.

72. The road into Denton village in the mid-1930's, still a charming suburb of Newhaven but much changed in the last thirty years. The 'Flying Fish' (or 'Kicking Donkey') can just be seen far right. Ralph Reader of Scout Gang Show Fame, came here as a young orphan and was raised by an uncle and aunt. His first job was a telegram boy at Newhaven and then he 'progressed' into the office of the Heighton Cement Works after the First World War. He left to work at another 'branch' in Ireland, from where he eventually travelled to America to live with an aunt who got him started on his theatrical road to fame.

73. Down they come! One chimney is being felled at the Heighton, Cement Works, Newhaven in the early 1920's. An advertising card regarding the Calstock Viaduct near Plymouth, reads: 'The whole of the Portland Cement used in the construction of the viaduct was manufactured and supplied by the Sussex Portland Cement Coy. Ltd., Newhaven, Sussex.' The quarry buildings became a munitions works during the First World War with numerous extra railway sidings being laid between the town station and the top of North Quay.

74. A must for the photo albums of the numerous lovers of Piddinghoe, the delightful village on the northern side of Newhaven. No longer a full rated village stores and now with an up-dated roof, this quaint building still turns most heads and cameras. The unique circular church steeple with its gilt fish weather vane, can be seen between the two houses (photo about 1887).

The Sussex Ouse at Piddinghoe

75. The topsail schooner 'Alert' about the 1920/30's discharges pig iron at Every's wharf, Piddinghoe.
The beauty of the scene speaks for itself, any changes can only spoil it.

76. Bishopstone Tidemills in August 1883. Without doubt the most popular view of the 'lost' village between Newhaven and the 'Buckle' Seaford. By this time the mill had become a Bonded warehouse purchased by the Harbour/Railway Coy., who had closed the creek (apart from two sluices) to enable the construction of East Quay. Using the flow of the tide and the release of pent up water on the ebb, it was claimed that the water wheels could turn for 16 hours out of the 24 daily. The workers communial laundry and their cottages are at the left as we here look towards the sea. Near right is Miller William Catt's house with the espalier pear trees. The sweeps of a windmill can be seen above, but in fact this was on the roof of the granary and was a wind driven crane for unloading and laoding barges which were floated *into* the building.